Faith for Increase

Bring a Positive Change Into Your Life by Exercising Your Faith

Pastor Chucks Uzonwanne
Christ House of Destiny Ministries
a.k.a. Voice of Bliss Outreach International

Faith for Increase

How to Exercise Your Faith

Chucks Uzonwanne

Christ House of Destiny Ministries
a.k.a. Voice of Bliss Outreach International

United Kingdom: Nigeria: USA:
Christ House of Destiny Ministries   Surulere, Lagos   Abingdon
Unity Hall, 144, Bramley Close   Tel: (00234)7028952010   Maryland 21009
Walthamstow   Tel: +4438238656
E17 6EG

E-mail: *christhouseofdestiny@yahoo.co.uk*
Website: *www.christhouseofdestiny.com*

This book was printed in Great Britain by Clays Ltd, St Ives plc

Rev. date: 05/18/2013

To order additional copies of this book, contact:
Xlibris Corporation
0-800-644-6988
www.xlibrispublishing.co.uk
Orders@xlibrispublishing.co.uk
306436

Contents

But these are written, that YE MIGHT BELIEVE THAT JESUS IS THE CHRIST, THE SON OF GOD; AND THAT BELIEVING YE MIGHT HAVE LIFE THROUGH HIS NAME.

(John 20:31)

THIS IS THE WORD OF FAITH WHICH
WE PREACH. If thou shall CONFESS WITH
THY MOUTH, the Lord Jesus and BELIEVE
IN YOUR HEART; that God hath raised him up
from the dead, THOU SHALL BE SAVED. For
WITH THE HEART MAN BELIEVETH UNTO
RIGHTEOUSNESS, AND WITH THE MOUTH,
CONFESSION IS MADE UNTO SALVATION.

(Romans 10:9-10)

COMMIT YOUR WORKS UNTO THE
LORD AND TRUST THEM WHOLLY TO
HIM; he will cause your thoughts to become
agreeable to his will, and SO SHALL YOUR
PLANS BE ESTABLISHED AND SUCCEED.

(Proverbs 16:3)

Acknowledgements

Foremost, I give thanks to the Most High God—Jehovah!
The creator and maker of all things who gave me the ability to put in
print this revelation.

My gratitude goes to the following:
Ifeoma and Josephine (my beloved sisters), without whose support and
encouragement I would not have been able to accomplish this project.

My mentors in the family of Christ whose tutelage and inspiration
encourage me still to exercise my faith!

To all friends and well-wishers, especially members of the Christ House
of Destiny Ministries and the Voice of Bliss Outreach International
production team.

Most importantly, Joan, who believed in and stood by me against all
odds, even when standing was not easy.

I say 'thank you' to all of you; may my God supply all your need
according to his riches in glory by Christ Jesus. Amen.

Preface

If we are looking to change hopeless situations, we need faith for increase. It is the only way to exercise our faith and to harness and actualise the promises of God for us.

This book is a collector's collection and a must-read! I certify and recommend this book for solution seekers who desire their faith life exercised and unleashed for increase.

—Pastor Chucks Uzonwanne

A road travelled by two makes a long distance short. The revelations in this book will be your converse to accompany, guide, and lead you on your journey to growth as you exercise your faith for increase.

—Pastor Chucks Uzonwanne

Introduction

THE TRUTHS IN this book will help you develop your faith and spiritual well-being. It will give you insights on how to overcome the challenges of life in your moments of trial through the application of your faith. It will position you for the good life and always encourage you to listen to the voice of the spirit and apply the word of God to seemingly impossible circumstances; it will bless and showcase you for greatness and for success if you will do what it says.

Know that whatever your circumstance, it is not beyond God to redeem and restore you; however, there is something you must also do, a part you must play for God to change that hopeless situation: 'You must put your faith to work by trusting in the Lord and by standing on his word always.' Don't see the problems, see God and see solutions, and believe in his word by exercising your faith. Start this instant, this minute; don't let go this opportunity to learn how to exercise and increase your faith.

They who put their trust in the Lord do not make haste; they're not anxious, and they want for nothing because the Lord is the source of their strength. Why not make the Lord the source of your strength and shake off the blur and be focused on the Author of your destiny. Put your trust in the Lord and don't be anxious. Make him your strength because that hopeless situation is your vantage point to start all over again and fulfil your destiny.

It is true that sometimes it is difficult to trust when you look at life issues especially when the odds are against you, considering the challenges that life brings. I am talking about the disappointments and betrayals from close associates that makes knowing who to trust difficult especially for someone at a cross road. Nevertheless, if you will trust in the Lord regardless of your experience and how you feel, he will mend your broken heart and bring you to the place of your fulfilment. You need to understand and realise that man may fail you, but when you trust in the Lord and acknowledge him in all your ways, he will direct your path and cause you to walk in high places. For he alone knows how to change times and seasons to benefit those who love him and are called according to his purpose.

If you are sick in your body, assuredly, he will bring healing to your whole body if you would let him? Because he is the Lord God your healer. And if you are poor and needy, remember, for your sake, he took your poverty that you might be rich. Jesus took your place and went on the cross for your sakes so you can be God's righteousness. Always remember, you have the right standing with him and he is with you, so take your place by exercising your faith in him and bring a positive change into your life. The power to make a positive change is within you only if you would look inwards to see; you've been endued with the dynamic ability to cause changes and recreate your world.

God desires for you to walk in your destiny and be fulfilled, and so, he wants to meet your needs if you will let him. He desires for you to have the good life knowing there is no failure in him; he is more than able to do exceeding, abundantly, above all that we may ask or think according to his power that is at work in us. However dismayed and disappointed you may be with man, always remember, there is One whose word is truth and never fails: He is Jehovah, the creator and maker of all things. His name is Jesus Christ. He is the King of kings and the Lord of lords. He is the Beginning and the End. He is the Alpha and the Omega, the Author and Perfecter of all faiths.

CHUCKS UZONWANNE

Summary
of
Introduction

Don't see the problems. See God and see solutions by
exercising your faith.

Ephesians 3:20

He is more than able to do exceeding, abundantly, above all that we
may ask or think according to his mighty power that is at work in us.

God is not a man, that He should lie, nor a son of man, that He should change His mind and repent. Does He speak and then not act? Does He promise and not fulfil?

(Numbers 23:19)

So shall my word be that goeth forth out of my mouth; it shall not return unto me void, but it shall accomplish that which I please, and it shall prosper in the thing whereto I sent it.

(Isaiah 55:11)

Receiving Through Faith

HAVE YOU EVER imagined reaching out with an outstretched arm to receive something from invisibility? The truth is that you can receive something from invisibility when you reach out in faith with the knowledge of the word of God and the understanding of who you are in Christ. Did you say, 'faith in the knowledge of the word of God? Yes, you need faith and the word of God to receive from invisibility because you are calling forth those things that be not as thou they were already in existence. This means you're operating from a higher realm where you can super impose on the natural. A higher realm is a spiritual vantage position where you can effect a positive change on the physical natural world. This is how faith works! Faith operates with the knowledge of the word of God. It accents and affirms the word of God to be true regardless of condition or circumstances because of its super imposition from a realm above the situation. Have a go and give it a try! Try reaching out to receive in faith and see that it is easy to receive when you apply your faith. What do you think?

For you must know, for you to conceive such thoughts will require absolute focus, this demands a conscious paying of attention, which means that you are consciously focusing all your energy to see from the perspective of God and applying your faith for the manifestation of your conceived thoughts.

This lets us know that faith adapts and is able to see clearly beyond human reasoning and insightfully reveals that faith expresses itself through focus because to be focused is to concentrate and pay particular attention to someone or something. Focus means to adapt, it is the state of producing clear vision by adjusting and adapting to the prevailing level of light. In other words, your faith has eyes to see into the realms and is able to receive from the realms of the spirit what the ordinary human eyes cannot see to be possible. This is why faith is an unseen reality because you're operating from a spiritual higher realms where only the supernatural takes place which is the significance for your operating with the eyes of the Spirit.

Faith is relative to prayer; they are synonymous and work pari passu! How do I mean? For instance, can you ask and not expect to receive? Which means you don't have faith because you're not in a state of anticipation; not being expectant and therefore don't believe? Know assuredly that the minute you ask believing you're putting your faith to work. Your expectation in this case is your place of observation that positions and puts you at a vantage point for faith to super-impose on nothingness based on your believing and desires. What do I mean by nothingness? Nothingness is the object of your meditation and desire. This is saying that your faith is activated the minute you ask believing. Are you implying that when I pray and ask for something, anything in consonance with the will of God and believe I have it that my faith is activated and ready to receive? Of course, yes! You've just said when it is in consonance with the will of God and when you believe that your faith will be activated. This is so, because it is predicated on the premise of you acting on your believing in faith. This insight is for you to know that faith is not believing and believing is not faith, but that they both work hand in hand to bring about reality. This makes it necessary for you to believe when you pray that God hears and answers, because all you need is to see your request with the eyes of faith and receive it. This makes prayer an important tool for faith to thrive.

In the same manner that prayer is a perceived consciousness of making the impossible possible, so faith and believing helps to make the possible a reality. And so, when you ask from God or someone, if you don't believe and have faith to receive, you will not receive because faith is a believer and a possessor. Faith makes the object of your desire real and keeps you believing for it until you possess it.

Another instance is, to walk with God and receive from him, the first step and foremost thing is for you to believe he exists by exercising your faith trusting that he is who he says he is. You must also believe that he desires for your needs to be met, that he hears and will answer when you ask because he is a faith God and faithful to his word.

Much of how we see things depends on how informed and knowledgeable we are, how we look at our surrounding circumstances and how we make our decisions. You must realise that your thought pattern is what makes you who you are; because as a man thinks in his heart, so is he. And so, when all you can see is trouble, challenges and the impossible, they become the determinant that informs your ability to solve problems and take decisions. This is so in the sense that the prognosis for the impossible is perspective prognosis for the impossible is perspective. Perspective is the understanding of the relative importance of things. It is a particular way of regarding something or the appearance of viewed objects with regard to other relative position. This allows us to turn the tables of crisis into moments of advantage based on our paradigm and decisions, for example, what you see to be impossible is possible with someone else. That it is impossible with you is because of the limit you have placed on yourself.

To achieve the impossible in adverse and hopeless situations, we need faith, focus, belief, and perspective. With these in mind, we can develop the right attitude and ways of perceiving our circumstances so as not to throw away or overlook the opportunity that comes with the crisis.

> [7]ASK, and IT SHALL BE GIVEN YOU; Seek, and you shall find;
> Knock and it shall be opened unto you: [8]For every one that Asketh
> RECEIVETH; and to him that knocketh it shall be Opened
> unto him.
>
> (Matthew 7:7-8)

These are the words of our Lord Jesus Christ on how you're to pray and receive—it reveals how you're to exercise your faith. These fundamental declarations are absolute truths with insights that will help us understand and discover who we are and the authority we've been given. It shows us how to receive through faith in the word of God!

To receive through faith, you must be able to stand on the word of God and believe that you have received what you asked for by acting and seeing you receiving those things you've asked for in faith according to God's promises and his perfect will for you.

What Makes You to Receive?

For verily I say unto you, that whosoever SHALL SAY unto this
mountain, Be thou removed, and be thou cast into the sea; and shall
not doubt in his heart, BUT SHALL BELIEVE THAT THOSE
THINGS WHICH HE SAITH SHALL COME TO PASS, HE
SHALL HAVE WHATSOEVER HE SAITH.

(Mark 11:23)

MANY TIMES, OUT of desperation, many people pray and don't
expect answers to their prayer; some even pray and can't remember
what they prayed about. This is because of anxiety and what they are going
through, these beclouds them and does not allow them to persist in prayer,
and to retain their request because they were not expecting an answer. So
they conclude that what will be will be, and so you have many of God's
children who have been praying for a long time for the same things without
receiving an answer to their prayers. Some are even praying and are praying
amiss and the wrong way; for these reasons and more, some have concluded
that God does not answer prayers; many have lost their faith as a result of
their unbelief and have backslid. Some have gone as far as concluding that
there is no God. What a shame!

When you listen to the way some people pray, you wonder if they are
praying to themselves or to the God above. Because they lack understanding
of his person and of the knowledge of the word of God, you would readily
know they're not students of the word of God and do not know who they
are. Many people pray and say the wrong things, and at some point, some
even cry and beg God to do for them what his word says belong to them.
For instance, someone says, 'O God, I have been crying and begging you
for my healing,' thinking if they cry and beg and say so, that would move
God and make him do what they want.

How can you cry and beg God for what he already says belong to
you: . . . for all things are yours (1 Corinthians 3:21). Knowing that what he
says belong to you is what he has given to you. What you need is 'knowledge
of his person', a firm relationship with him. If you will soak yourself in the

word and let it gain ascendancy in your spirit, you will be amazed at what your faith can accomplish.

Another says, 'O God, I have been begging you to give me a child.' Or, 'O God, I have been praying and begging you for money since.' These are all wrong ways to pray if we are to exercise our faith and get results; it is not the right way to ask and receive from God. A thousand times no, it isn't!

I know it is not the right way to exercise your faith because I also have been ignorant at some point and prayed once like this: 'O God, where are you in this situation?' 'Why is this happening to me, why me?' Does this sound familiar to you? If it does sound familiar to you, what did you do? Seeking attention and thinking it would change anything would not. It never did in my case until I woke up, propped myself, and held on to prayer, my faith and the word of God. The revelation I got that propped me to my feet was as a result of my questions and the answer I got in return, 'if not you who else has its time come for upliftment' and like a thunderbolt, this answer was a rude awakening that jolted and steered me instantly to see the good in the bad situation. And so, I took advantage of the situation and yielded myself to the leading of the Holy Spirit of God. It is expedient for you to know that in circumstances when all is lost, there is the need for you to persistently pray, resolutely hold on to your faith and the word of God. This would help your focus, your perspective and the ability for you to hear the voice of the Spirit of God.

You see I dealt with such ignorance a long time ago when I got a revelation of what I should have been saying and doing with my faith. This is why I'm sharing this with you so you can put your faith to work. The word of God is active and powerful when rightly applied in obedience and in faith because it is infallible and immutable. If you would like to know what I did to turn around the situation for good, and more about the prayer of faith and the right way to pray, get the book I wrote titled *The Power of Prayer*. It will help you discover your prayer-life, encourage you to get answers to your prayers, and position you to walk in victory and in dominion. Plus that, it will reveal who you truly are and will put your destiny in your hands.

Many of the challenges children of God are facing is ignorance of the word of God and lack of faith, which means they lack the ability to look firstly, inward in themselves in moments of adversity and secondly, up to God for his promises because of an impaired and obscured vision. They lack the ability to see beyond the earth realm and so they walk on in unbelief and in darkness. If only they will introspect and look to observe with the eyes of the spirit to behold the light of their redemption, darkness will elude them and not becloud them. When the cosmic rays of life is beamed on a human person; when that God's light of redemption gains entrance into your heart and ascend into your spirit, of a necessity darkness will be dispelled and every chain of the enemy will be broken and you will be made free. For the entrance of God's word gives light and understanding; it makes the one whose gaze is fixated and predetermined to arise and shine with the glory of God.

Let's look at some scriptures that will enable us to see the light and understand how to stand strong in the face of opposition. With these scriptures, we will be strengthened in faith when we pray and speak words with tremendous power that will make us to receive from God when our faith is put to work.

> [19]And being NOT WEAK IN FAITH, he (Abraham) considered not his own body now dead, when he was about a hundred years old, neither yet the deadness of Sarah's womb: [20]He staggered not at the promise of God through unbelief; but was STRONG IN FAITH, GIVING GLORY TO GOD.
>
> (Romans 4:19-20)

These scriptures in consideration let us know that Abraham was not weak in his faith. He considered not what he was seeing and experiencing physically speaking, but was strong in faith giving glory to God because he immovably and uncompromisingly held on to the promises of God.

In the same manner, every believer must be strengthened in their faith and remain immovable and uncompromising on the promises of God inspite of their circumstances. You might be reading this book for various reasons, but whatever your reason, what you need is to be strengthened in your faith and keep on holding on to the promises of God. That situation cannot defeat you as long as you're a child of God, because it has not come to stay, but will surely come to pass with your victory and a smile on your face if only you will not stagger and consider the circumstances.

> For verily I say unto you, that whosoever SHALL SAY unto this mountain, Be thou removed, and be thou cast into the sea; and shall not doubt in his heart, BUT SHALL BELIEVE THAT THOSE THINGS WHICH HE SAITH SHALL COME TO PASS, HE SHALL HAVE WHATSOEVER HE SAITH.
>
> (Mark 11:23)

CHUCKS UZONWANNE

ASK, and IT SHALL BE GIVEN YOU; seek, and you shall find;
Knock and it shall be opened unto you: For every one that
Asketh RECEIVETH; and to him that knocketh it shall be
Opened unto him.

(Matthew 7:7-8)

This reveals to us the need to be strong in faith—that when we ask, we should believe we have what we have asked for and then receive; evidently for you to receive, you must 'ask', 'say', 'pray'; believe that those things which you saith shall come to pass, and you shall have 'receive' whatsoever you saith.

This is letting us know the procedure for exercising our faith when we pray. Before and after you 'ask, say, or pray', you must *believe* in the word of God that what you've prayed about was heard and answered by God, and then *receive* in *faith*. Just receive! It is at the point of *receipt* that the manifestation becomes real and yours. The point of receipt is when your faith has been activated and put to work and gotten a response; you can only know you've gotten a response if you are a person of faith and this will be revealed by the promptings in your spirit, this is when the possession is yours, and available to you. But you must also act on your believing, knowing within you that you have gotten it.

What a revelation! If you have an understanding of what this is saying, you will know you don't need to cry and beg God for anything! It is the constant exercising of your faith, the right declaration of what you say, and the receipt of your believing that gets your prayers answered. So stop the beggarly life! Stop crying and begging for what belongs to you.

1 Corinthians 3:21 say, 'All things are yours,' meaning all things have been freely given to us in Christ Jesus (Romans 8:32). God giveth us richly all things to enjoy (1 Timothy 6:17), because all things are working together for good to them who love God, who are called according to his purpose (Romans 8:28). If only you will stop begging, crying and worrying, and earnestly begin to pray, exercise your faith and also thanking the Lord for what he has began in your life; knowing that he who has begun a good work in you will definitely accomplish and perfect it. This means that prosperity is yours! Healing is yours! Divine health is yours! Success and greatness belongs to you in Christ Jesus. There is nothing we desire according to the will of God, that we cannot have when we apply our faith and pray the right way with gratitude in our heart.

Listen to what 2 Peter 1:3 says, maybe it will help you come out of that abyss of despondency and clear your blurry eyes: 'According as his divine power hath given unto us all things that pertain unto life and godliness, and through the knowledge of him that hath called us unto glory and virtue.'

How can you know this and still resort to a beggarly life? You are not only making yourself insignificant, you are nullifying the word of God in your life and rendering yourself ineffective, inoperative, and making yourself an unbeliever. Don't make yourself inoperative and ineffective with unbelief because God's divine ability is at work in you to prove his word in your life and make you proclaim your rights in Christ. This is why he has given you all things that pertain unto life and godliness. You must realise that through his knowledge, he has called you unto his glory and virtue for his marvellous light to shine providence through you. This is why all things work together for good to them who love God, who are called according to his purpose. Did you hear him say 'something'? No, but all things! All things are working together for your good. Settle it in your heart that that situation is working together for your good. This is the confident assurance of faith that we have in him!

If you are in need of money, don't beg for money; just keep declaring to yourself, 'Money comes to me now in the name of Jesus, I have money to meet my needs,' believe it and stand on your faith! But you must also do something legitimate that God would use as a channel to make money available unto you. You must use your gifts and utilise your time! Do something, work and be where God has destined for you by discovering your calling in life, and be a blessing to your generation.

If you are sick, infirmed, or diseased in your body, don't cry and beg God for your healing; confess what the word says about your healing, 'By his stripes, I am healed,' personalise and believe it, and receive your healing by exercising your faith in the name of Jesus! You must believe it for your faith to receive it. Search the scriptures for God's word that deals on healing and apply them appropriately to yourself.

If you have complications in your body, or are barren and are in need for a child, don't cry and beg God for a child; come before God based on his promises, and go get the scriptures on the matter at hand and declare it. Say, 'Father, I thank you for I've received a male or a female child just like you answered the prayer of Hannah concerning Samuel, so I receive, in the name of Jesus.' This must depend on your desire as you take God's word to him, and keep declaring and saying what his word says.

'Children are the heritage of the Lord, and the fruit of the womb is his reward' (Psalm 127:3). Then pray like this: 'I thank you Father for making my womb fruitful and to conceive my male or female child according to your word, in Jesus' name.' Insert your name where necessary and keep saying it to yourself! It doesn't matter for how long you confess it, just keep saying it, keep saying it until it gains residency in your spirit, and until you can see it in the realms of the spirit.

Say this: 'Lord, I'm also standing in faith on your word that says, "You will be blessed more than any other people; none of your men or women will be childless, nor any of your livestock without young"' (Deuteronomy 7:14). Insert your name as you make your declarations.

'Thy wife shall be as a fruitful vine by the sides of thy house: thy children like olive plants round about thy table' (Psalm 128:3). Say, my wife is a fruitful vine. She is fertile and productive, and bears goodly sons and daughters in the mighty name of Jesus, Amen.

Therefore, I reverse all impossibilities that stand in the way of me having children as I call forth all that pertain to life and godliness; I call forth my sons and daughters (children) in the mighty name of Jesus. I decree prosperity in my life, in my home, and in the works of my hand, and I walk in strength, I live in divine health, and I have sound mind. I call forth my destiny in greatness and in success, in the mighty name of our Lord and saviour Jesus Christ. Amen.

Speaking like this in faith will cause the Spirit of God's word to produce what it says in your life because God's word has taken abode in your spirit. When the Spirit of God takes hold of a man, he brings an excellent, prominent and notable transformation, glory to God!

It is your responsibility to study the word of God and know the blessings of God for you. It is also your responsibility to meditate regularly on the word by spending time in the presence of God and carefully measuring your thoughts with the word of God, gauge it, and say those things as it concerns you in the name of Jesus. Can you feel your faith rising? This is the very essence for which you're reading this book. Your faith is rising because it is being activated as a result of the word you're hearing and your spirit bears witness with the Spirit of the word of God because you now believe. This is what acting on your believing is. When you awake and arise and begin to do the supernaturally uncommon as a result of the word you're hearing. This is because the word has gained ascendancy in your spirit and is now building you up for your predestined great destiny. Imagine someone behind the wheel of an automobile car, who ignites the engine of the car and puts the gear of the car in forwards motion and begins to accelerate the car with his foot on the throttle increasingly as the moment go by; of a necessity the speed level of the car will increase with every acceleration. In similar manner, your faith finds increase in the word. It is increased with every word of God you ingest and digest, and as you keep on believing and acting out your believe in faith, assuredly, it will produce results. This is how to exercise your faith for increase.

Now that you have believed, all you need is to *receive* those things that are yours in Christ Jesus. You can start by declaring, 'I have peace in my life and in my home and I walk in love and in joy. Salvation is mine in Christ Jesus because the Bible says, "What saith it, the word is near you, in your heart and in your mouth, the word of faith which we preach. If thou shall confess with thy mouth, the Lord Jesus and believe in your heart; that God hath raised him up from the dead, thou shall be saved. For with the heart man believeth unto righteousness, and with the mouth, confession is made unto salvation"' (Romans 10:8-10).

I therefore, decree and declare that divine health and peace are mine because the Bible says, 'But he was wounded for our transgressions, he was bruised for our iniquities; the chastisement of our peace was upon him; and with his stripes we are healed' (Isaiah 53:5).

You must of necessity personalize your confessions for it to take root and have effect in your spirit and in your life. Now, get ready to apply yourself in the scriptures below as you confess and put your faith to work to possess the object of your desire.

So you say, 'But he was wounded for my transgression, he was bruised for my iniquity; the chastisement of my peace was upon him; and with his stripes I [Mr/Mrs/Miss—] am healed' (Isaiah 53:5).

'Who his own self bare our [my] sins in his own body on the tree that we [I], being dead to sins, should live unto righteousness: by whose stripes you [I was] were healed' (1 Peter 2:24).

Prosperity is mine; I am fruitful and productive because the Bible says, 'He is [I am] like a tree planted by streams of water which yields its fruit in season and whose leaf does not wither. Whatever he does [I do] prospers' (Psalm 1:3).

'⁷Most blessed is the man who believes in, trusts in, and relies on the lord, and whose hope and confidence the Lord is. ⁸For he shall be like a tree planted by the waters that spreads out its roots by the river; and it shall not see and fear when heat comes; but its leaf shall be green. It shall not be anxious and full of care in the year of drought, nor shall it cease yielding fruit' (Jeremiah 17:7-8).

Exercise your faith some more and keep declaring and seeing you walking in your victory, glory to God! Now keep declaring, confessing, and saying by appropriating the scriptures to yourself: 'Success is mine, greatness and victory are mine in Christ Jesus because the Bible declares concerning me, "And he [I] sought God in [mine day] the days of Zechariah, who had [I who has] understanding in the visions of God: and as long as he [I seek] sought the Lord, God made him [makes me] to prosper—succeed"' (2 Chronicles 26:5).

The Bible says, 'Commit your works unto the Lord and trust them wholly to him; he will cause your thoughts to become agreeable to his will, and so shall your plans be established and succeed' Proverbs 16:3.

'May God give you the desire of your heart and make all your plans to succeed' (Psalm 20:4).

Jehoshaphat stood and said, 'Hear me, O Judah, and you inhabitants of Jerusalem; believe in the Lord your God, so shall you be established; believe his prophets, so shall you prosper—to Succeed' (2 Chronicles 20:20).

But my God shall supply all your need according to his riches in glory by Christ Jesus (Philippians 4:19). Now insert your name in the scriptures above meditatingly, and keep on confessing to yourself until you're completely immersed with faith and believing to the intent that you're sold out to your confessions, exuding that confident assurance that the object of your desire is yours. At this point your faith is in full motion to bring your desires to reality for your possession.

As you keep declaring God's truth to yourself in that situation, you will discover your faith beginning to rise more and more, and every weight holding you down will be dropped and peace from above will be on the increase within you as you keep on exercising your faith.

As you call forth those things you desire, believe they're yours and see them manifesting and as long as you receive them in your spirit, they will become yours. It doesn't matter what your physical surrounding is saying or how you feel about or regarding what your optical eyes and senses dictates; just keep your eyes of faith focused on the object of your desire, it's a matter of time the inevitable will become visible.

Do you have a relationship with God? Are you his bona fide child? Would you categorically say, 'I am born-again and I know the Lord as my saviour,' and witness his love to your sphere of contact? If you have answered no to all these questions, there is still hope for you.

All you need is Jesus Christ and your only hopes is saying 'Yes' to him and receive him into your life. Acknowledge you are a sinner and confess thus, 'In the name of Jesus, Father, here and now I acknowledge and forsake my sins. I receive Jesus Christ as my Lord and Saviour, and take the Holy Bible as your Living Word to me. I renounce my old ways of life and every work of darkness in my life.'

The Bible says if I confess with my mouth the Lord Jesus and believe in my heart that God has raised him from the dead, I shall be saved. For with the heart, man believes unto righteousness, and with the mouth, confession is made unto salvation.

I believe and therefore confess that Jesus Christ died for my sins on the cross of Calvary and rose from the dead on the third day. He shed his precious blood for the remittance of my sin. The Bible says, if any man be in Christ, he is a new creation, old things have passed away; behold, all things have become new.

Thank you, Father, for saving me and giving me a new life in Christ as I work in the light of your righteousness and live holy and a victorious life. Henceforth, I declare I'm a child of God, born of God's Spirit; I have the life of God in me and the Spirit of the Son of God is at work in me, and I have dominion, sound mind, and I live in divine health in the name of Jesus. Amen.

Summary
of
'What Makes You to Receive?'

These fundamental declarations are absolute truths that will help you understand and discover who you are and the authority you've been given.

Matthew 7:7-8
Mark 11:23
Romans 4:19-20

How can you know this and still resort to a beggarly life? You are not only making yourself insignificant, you are nullifying the word of God in your life and rendering yourself ineffective, inoperative, and making yourself an unbeliever

---

It is also your responsibility to meditate, to carefully measure your thoughts with the word of God, gauge it, and keep saying those things as it concerns you always.

What Is the Promise For?

I T IS CRUCIAL to define the meaning of a promise! This is imperative if we're to understand what promises are for. So, what is a promise? A promise is a pledge that commits oneself to a certain course of action. It is an assurance that one will do something or that something will happen. An indication that something is likely to occur, which means, it is a source of hope, and basis for expectations. It is a declaration of intention. It means to give one's word and uphold it. It also means to vow and bring it to pass.

A promise from God is given to me so that I may know intelligently what God has deposited in my account; this commits me to a certain course of action. It is a source of hope and basis for my expectations because of what God has planned for me, his thoughts for me, and how he wants me to live my future. It is a declaration of God's intention because it tells me what God will give me and makes me know what to claim. This is an assurance that he will do what he says he will do when he will do it because he has given his word. His word is his promise, which he will uphold and bring to pass at his appointed time.

"'For I know the thoughts and plans I have for you," declares the Lord, "thoughts and plans to prosper you and not to harm, of peace and not of evil, to give you hope and a good future'" (Jeremiah 29:11).

A promise from God is his word that reminds me of his immutability, his infallibility, indestructibility, incorruptible and eternal. This is faith and knowledge resting on the hope of (God's word} eternal life, which God, who does not lie, promised before the beginning of time, and at his appointed season brought his word to light through preaching. Speaking of God, the Bible says, "By myself I have sworn, my mouth has uttered in all integrity a word that will not be revoked (Isaiah 45: 23; Titus 1: 2- 3). "Don't be deceived, my dear brothers. Every good and perfect gift is from above, coming down from the Father of the heavenly lights, who does not change like shifting shadows (James 1: 16 - 17; Numbers 23: 19; Malachi 3: 6; 1 Samuel 15: 29). Our God does not change, he is Sovereign and Truth, which is why he declares: So is my word that goes out from my mouth: it will not return to me empty, but will accomplish what I desire and achieve the purpose for which I sent it (Isaiah 55: 11). How do I know God's promises for me? The word of God contains God's promises to his children. And so, for me to know God's promises, I would have to revert to his word to know what his word says concerning me and apply his word to my life, to actualise his promises for me. When I stand on the word in faith regardless of the circumstances and apply God's word to that situation because I know what he has promised concerning me in his word. If my resolve is to stand on his word trustingly, then I am holding on to the promises of God. How do you hold on to the promises of God? You hold on to the promises of God by standing on the word of God in faith and by applying the word to that situation and believing God trustingly, uncompromisingly and immoveable that regardless of the dictates of your senses, it will turn out right. That is, you're not moved by how you feel, neither are you moved by what you see nor are you moved by what you hear because you believe the word of God has gone forth and surely must accomplish its desire on the matter. This is exactly what Abraham did; he believed the word of God and held on to God's promises regardless of his circumstances.

Therefore, It behoves us to conclude that promises are intelligent directions that rest upon the character and ability of God for faith to possess its possessions. God's promises are the means he uses to chart the course of our lives and bring his word concerning us to pass. It gives us confidence to rest on the ores of God that he is definitely who he says he is!

Consider the following:

> God is not a man, that he should lie, nor a son of man, that he
> should change his mind. Does he speak and then not act? Does he
> promise and not fulfil?
>
> (Numbers 23:19)

When Balaam uttered those wonderful words to Balak concerning the children of Israel and God, seldom did he know what he was saying because it was by the leading of the Spirit of God that he was able to prophesy such great words. This is prove positive that God upholds his promises to his children. Here they were, the Israelites having left Egypt and where passing through Moab in the wilderness to Canaan, the land of their promise, but Balak the king of Moab would not allow them passage because he was afraid of them. He wanted them cursed and put in confusion, so, he summoned Balaam, a Prophet to curse the Israelites, but because God had promised to lead the Israelites, he would not allow them to be cursed by anyone because of his promise. God's character is immutable and synonymous with his word ; this is because he is not a man that he should alter his word once spoken nor can he change his mind at the hour of need.

> So shall my word be that goeth forth out of my mouth; it shall not
> return unto me void, but it shall accomplish that which I please, and
> it shall prosper in the thing whereto I sent it.
>
> (Isaiah 55:11)

The above instances reveal the person of God and his character. He makes us know that when he speaks, he will fulfil his promises. It shows he watches over his word by making sure that his promises to us are fulfilled regardless of the troubles of the moment because he is not a man that he should lie about his thoughts and plans to grant us salvation and bless us when we obey him and do what he expects from us. He is who he says he is and will not change!

Summary
of
'What Is the Promise For?'

Numbers 23:19
Isaiah 55:11

A promise is given to me so that I may know intelligently what God has deposited in my account, what he has planned for me, his thoughts for me, and how he wants me to live my future.

God's promises are the means he uses to chart the course of our lives and bring his word concerning us to pass. It gives us confidence to rest on the ores of God that he is who he says he is!

---

¹⁹And being NOT WEAK IN FAITH, he considered not his own body now dead, when he was about an hundred years old, neither yet the deadness of Sarah's womb:
²⁰HE STAGGERED NOT AT THE PROMISES OF GOD THROUGH UNBELIEF,
But was STRONG IN FAITH, GIVING GLORY TO GOD;
²¹And BEING FULLY PERSUADED that, WHAT GOD HAD PROMISED, HE WAS ABLE ALSO TO PERFORM.

(Romans 4:19-21)

Now faith is being sure of what we hope for and certain of what we do not see.

(Hebrews 11:1, NIV)

Now faith is the assurance [the confirmation, the title deed] of the things [we] hope for, being the proof of things [we] do not see and the conviction of their reality [faith perceiving as real fact what is not revealed to the senses].

(Hebrews 11:1, Amplified Bible)

CHUCKS UZONWANNE

Now faith is the substance of things hoped for, the evidence of things not seen.

(Hebrews 11:1, KJV)

What Is Faith?

FAITH IS UNSEEN reality. It perceives as fact what is not revealed to the senses. This means it overrides every sense of limit and doubt, and conceives the desires of the one whose faith is at work and presents as reality the conceived desire for his believing and possession. It is acting on what you believe that which you see with the eyes of the spirit. Faith makes what you say and decree concerning what you see in the realms of the Spirit to become real and yours as a result of your believing. This is laying hold on your inheritance based on your insight and the knowledge of God's word. Faith is seeing the unseen; this is so because faith is a believer and a possessor. The unseen is the realm of the existence of faith; it is seeing with the eyes of the Spirit of God!

> While we look not at the things which are seen, but at the things
> which are not seen; for the things which are seen are temporary;
> but the things which are not seen are eternal.
>
> (2 Corinthians 4:18)

This scripture we've just read does not say, 'we look not', it is saying that we look only at the things which the ordinary human eyes cannot fathom or comprehend because of where we live, where we're operating from, our life style of faith. You must bear in mind that these things that we look at can only be seen with the eyes of faith. So our operations are not manmade, neither are they physical but mighty through God to the pulling down of strong holds casting down imaginations that are not aligned in obedience to the word of God, or any distracting thing that stands in the way of our faith. These are eternal verities which only the initiated can relate with as tangible realities because they're mysterious and can only be spiritually discerned. So, when you look, what do you see? It matters what you see! Do you look and see with the eyes of faith? or do you look with your optical eyes and see only the earth realm? Are you asking what I mean by 'seeing with the eyes of faith' which means you have not been paying attention to all we've been saying. It matters where your heart is and what you look at, and most importantly, if you see what you're supposed to see because looking and seeing are two different things entirely. If you would pay attention, you would not look with your optical eyes what you're supposed to look with the eyes of faith because chances are that you'll not see what you're intended to see. This will cause you to become motionless, immobilised and directionless because you're looking and seeing the wrong things. These wrong things will work against you because they deal with your senses and will negate the word of God in your life. This can only inspire fear and doubt which means you're incapacitated and ineffective and cannot exercise your faith. Because of your incapacitation and inoperativeness, what you need is spiritual eye-salve with which you can look to see correctly. Reason being that where there is no vision the people perish. This is the more reasons you need to exercise your faith and look with the eyes of the Spirit to be able to comprehend the promises of God for you, so you can possess your possessions.

Faith is a possessor! Jesus said, 'For verily I say unto you, that WHOSOEVER SHALL SAY unto this mountain, be thou removed, and be thou cast into the sea, and shall not doubt in his heart, but shall BELIEVE THAT THOSE THINGS WHICH HE SAITH SHALL COME TO PASS, **HE SHALL HAVE WHATSOEVER HE SAITH.'**
(Mark 11:23)

Now faith is being sure of what we hope for and certain of what we do not see. It is the assurance, the confirmation, the title deed of the things we hope for, being the proof of things we do not see and the conviction of their reality. Faith perceives as real fact what is not revealed to the senses.
(Hebrews 11:1)

Clearly, faith is an organ of knowledge that does not doubt any sense of reason, but would not allow sense of reason to stand in its way of supernatural accomplishment. In other words, faith believes in sense of reason, it considers the fact at hand but does not allow the fact in hand or sense of reason to dictate its supernatural existence because faith is a super imposer; it calls forth those things from the realms of the spirit that cannot be seen with the optical eyes (sense of reason) as though they are physically in existence.

This means that the person who has put his faith, confidence, boldness, assurance, and trust in God has access to knowledge that the natural sense of reason cannot have because faith ignores reason and rises above it.

Faith in God is not dependent upon the support of any sense of reason; faith goes straight into the presence of God to receive and bring into manifestation for the possession of the one whose faith is at work, which truly suggests that faith is indeed an unseen reality and it calls forth those things that are not into existence.

Faith is a declaration of what belongs to you because it depends on God's character; it rests in the confidence of the one who made the promises. Faith is walking in the footsteps of God and doing exactly what he says and does.

The Bible says that Abraham did not waver in his faith through unbelief regarding the promises of God, but was strong (strengthened) in his faith and gave glory to God, being fully persuaded that God had power to do what he had promised. This means that Abraham didn't consider the physical-ness of his body, but held on to God's promises by putting his faith to work and constantly giving glory to God. Let's read it in Romans 4:19-21:

> [19]And being NOT WEAK IN FAITH, he considered not his own body now dead, when he was about an hundred years old, neither yet the deadness of Sarah's womb:
> [20]HE STAGGERED NOT AT THE PROMISES OF GOD THROUGH UNBELIEF,
> But was STRONG IN FAITH, GIVING GLORY TO GOD;
> [21]And BEING FULLY PERSUADED that, WHAT GOD HAD PROMISED,
> HE WAS ABLE ALSO TO PERFORM.

Summary
of
'What Is Faith?'

Faith is an organ of knowledge that does not doubt any sense of reason, but would not allow sense of reason to stand in its way of supernatural accomplishment.

---

2 Corinthians 4:18
Mark 11:23
Romans 4:19-21

Faith is unseen reality. It is acting on what you believe that which you see with the eyes of the spirit. What you say and decree concerning what you see becomes yours because your faith is at work.

The Importance of Faith

ANYTHING THAT HAS no value does not demand much of attention. This is because value placed on a thing is the yard stick for measuring its importance. To measure the importance of one's faith therefore will be determined by how much the person is willing to see with the eyes of faith. Let's not throw over-board the fact that faith is unseen reality, a super-imposer and a sister to believing. This means having a relationship and a walk with God, coupled with the fact that faith is a possessor. These are some of the factors that make faith important and a value that cannot be over-emphasised. How strong is your faith, and how much do you desire for your faith to be effective and make a difference in your prayer life? And how important is your faith to you?

These questions would help to inform you, and catapult your faith, and grant you the desire to discover and make your faith to be effective as you work towards exercising your faith for increase:

> [19]Then came the disciples to Jesus apart, and said, why could not we cast him out? [20]And Jesus said unto them, because of your unbelief [of the littleness of your faith]; for verily I say unto you, if ye have faith as a grain of mustard seed, ye shall say unto this mountain, remove hence to yonder place; and it shall remove; and nothing shall be impossible unto you.[21]Howbeit this kind goeth not out but by prayer and fasting.
>
> (Matthew 17:19-21)

Here was an opportunity for the disciples of Jesus to prove their mettle, having heard Jesus preach so much on faith and also operated his own faith and have gotten amazing results. But, it so happens that the faith of the disciples were little and weak because it could not accomplish their desire. They desired for the boy to be healed, but lack the impetus to activate their faith and make it work. The Lord Jesus made it clear why they could not exercise their faith and heal the boy—because of their unbelief and the fact that they lacked prayer. Unbelief is a killer of faith that will rob you of an effective prayer life. Unbelief is related to impossibility; these will limit your ability to see with the eyes of faith and will hinder you from being able to call forth the object of your desire and bring them into reality. It will make you unable to possess your possession because you will not be able to decree a thing and bring it to pass where you don't believe and see it to be possible. The Bible makes it clear that the disciples of Jesus tried to heal the lunatic [epileptic] boy, but they could not. The prove of Jesus' Lordship is that when he came on the scene, he healed the boy and went further to explain to the disciples why they could not heal the boy. Simply that they were unbelieving and lacked faith, prayer and fasting. I need you to understand something here, they desired for the boy to be healed but didn't have 'faith'; the pre-requisites and requirement for the boy's healing. It didn't matter that they were many, since none of them had faith, it made no difference because Jesus said unto them, because of your unbelief [of the littleness of your faith]; for verily I say unto you, if ye have faith as a grain of mustard seed, ye shall say unto this mountain, remove hence to yonder place; and it shall remove; and nothing shall be impossible unto you. Another revelation in all of these is if you have faith lika a grain of mustard seed, you can move your mountain and nothing shall be impossible unto you. Did you also notice that unbelief and impossibility were mentioned in the scripture as hindrances to the faith of the disciples? As a believer, under no circumstance should you allow unbelief to cripple your faith nor should you allow impossibility to dominate and limit you from accomplishing the object of your desire.

Contrast the scene above with that of the woman with the issue of blood who understood the importance of her faith and needn't no one to stand in her way.

> [20]And behold, a woman, which was diseased with an issue of blood
> twelve years, came behind him [Jesus], and touched the hem of
> his garment: [21]For she said within herself, if I may but touch his
> garment, I shall be whole. [22]But Jesus turned him about, and when
> he saw her, he said, Daughter, be of good comfort; thy faith hath
> made thee whole. And the woman was made whole from that hour.
> (Matthew 9:20-22)

The Bible makes us to understand that because she believed and kept on confessing her desire for her healing, that triggered her faith into action as she walked towards Jesus for a touch of the helm of his garment; this catapulted her into her healing. She put her faith to work, believing in herself that Jesus was able to heal her at the touch of the helm of his garment and that made her whole according to the words of our Lord Jesus.

[25]And a certain woman, which had an issue of blood twelve years,
[26]And had suffered many things of many physicians, and had spent all that she had, and was nothing bettered, but rather grew worse,
[27]WHEN SHE HAD HEARD OF JESUS, CAME IN THE PRESS BEHIND, AND TOUCHED HIS GARMENT. [28]FOR SHE SAID, IF I MAY TOUCH BUT HIS CLOTHES, I SHALL BE WHOLE. [29]AND STRAIGHTWAY THE FOUNTAIN OF HER BLOOD WAS DRIED UP; AND SHE FELT IN HER BODY THAT SHE WAS HEALED OF THAT PLAGUE.
[30]And Jesus immediately knowing in himself that virtue had gone out of him, turned him about in the press, and said, who touched my clothes? . . . [33]But the woman fearing and trembling, knowing what was done in her, came and fell down before him, and told him all the truth. [34]And he said unto her, Daughter, thy faith hath made the whole; go in peace, and be whole of thy plague.

(Mark 5:25-34)

The book of Mark gives a more detailed account and insight of the case of the woman with the issue of blood. She had suffered in the hands of doctors and had spent all the money she had. The Bible says, 'She was nothing bettered, but rather grew worse.'

Her hope was resurrected and strengthened when she heard of Jesus and his healing powers, and she went amidst the multitude of people that were touching Jesus and touched the hem of his garment with a touch of her faith. Can you imagine how high her hopes were when she saw Jesus and quickly ceased the opportunity to take advantage of the situation and exercised her faith? The Bible says, 'and straightway the fountain of her blood was dried up; and she felt in her body that she was healed of that plague.'

Her healing was of faith because Jesus perceived in spite of the multitude thronging him that someone had touched him with the exercise of faith and pulled out power from him. The Bible lets us know that she was able to carry out this act of faith when she heard about Jesus and believed in her heart for her healing.

Have you heard about Jesus? What are you going to do with the name of Jesus? And what are you doing with the word of God you're hearing?

The remarkable thing worthy of note is that she wasn't asking the Lord Jesus to pray for her, or touch her nor look in her direction. She did not desire any such attention, no, but she kept saying within her, 'If I only touch his garment, I shall be restored to health.' She kept on confessing her belief and sought for an opportunity to exercise her faith, and as her opportunity came, she put her faith to work and got her confession, glory be to God.

It is very important to understand the operations of faith; firstly, the woman conceived what she wanted, kept on confessing it, and acted at the fullness of her believing. As she unleashed her faith, this made her faith to soar above all opposition and doubt and she possessed the object of her desire because she had strong faith.

Her resolve was to exercise her faith; her mind was made up to receive her healing as she built her faith to increase with her confessions regardless of the danger she would face when caught by the Jewish leaders, because traditionally, according to the Jewish culture she was not supposed to be seen in public as a result of her condition, but she undermined the consequences and put her faith to work.

And Jesus, knowing in himself that virtue, power had gone out of him when she reached out in faith and touched the hem of his garment, asked who touched me and looked about to see her who had exercised her faith, for he said to her, 'Daughter, thy faith hath made thee whole; go in peace, and be whole of thy plague.'

Picture the scenario and see the woman, who once was helpless and could not be helped by the doctors and those who knew her, frenzied and jubilant, overwhelmed, and ecstatic with joy as she experienced a miracle in her body, watching her body condition change, the same body that the doctors could do nothing about was healed, glory be to God.

Where are you in your life? Do you need the exercise of your faith to prop you up and bring you into your inheritance? Then now is the time, go ahead and confess your believing, exercise your faith in prayer and possess your possessions.

For ye are all the CHILDREN OF GOD BY
FAITH IN CHRIST JESUS.

(Galatians 3:26)

I am crucified with Christ: nevertheless I live; yet not I, but Christ liveth in me; and the life which I now live in the flesh I LIVE BY THE FAITH OF THE SON OF GOD, who loved me, and gave himself for me.

(Galatians 2:20)

But WITHOUT FAITH IT IS IMPOSSIBLE TO PLEASE GOD: for him that cometh to God must believe that he is, and that he is a rewarder of them that diligently seek him.

(Hebrews 11:6)

Why Do We Need Faith?

WE NEED FAITH because of the following:

1. We are saved (justified) by faith through Christ Jesus:

Therefore BEING JUSTIFIED BY FAITH, we have peace with God
THROUGH OUR LORD JESUS CHRIST: [2]BY WHOM ALSO
WE HAVE ACCESS BY FAITH INTO THIS GRACE WHEREIN
WE STAND, and rejoice in hope of the glory of God.
(Romans 5:1-2)

For ye are all the CHILDREN OF GOD BY FAITH IN
CHRIST JESUS
(Galatians 3:26)

THAT CHRIST MAY DWELL IN YOUR HEARTS BY FAITH.
(Ephesians 3:17)

2. We must live by faith in Christ Jesus because we have been justified
by faith:

I am crucified with Christ: nevertheless I live; yet not I, but Christ
liveth in me; and the life which I now live in the flesh I LIVE BY
THE FAITH OF THE SON OF GOD, who loved me, and gave
himself for me.
(Galatians 2:20)

NOW THE JUST SHALL LIVE BY FAITH.
(Hebrews 10:38a)

For therein is THE RIGHTEOUSNESS OF GOD REVEALED
FROM FAITH TO FAITH: as it is written, the just shall live by faith
(Romans 1:17)

For whatsoever is born of God overcometh the world: and this is
the VICTORY THAT OVERCOMETH THE WORLD,
EVEN OUR FAITH

(1 John 5:4)

3. We cannot please God without faith because we need faith to believe
    in the existence of God. How can we prove that God exists? In as
    much as we need a revelation to understand the person of God;
    his creation is a prove that he exists. He made the heavens and
    the earth, the moon, stars, galaxies, the milky way, etc. Hear what
    testimony the Bible gives of him: [25]To whom then will you liken
    me, or shall I be equal? Saith the Holy one. [26]Lift up your eyes on
    high, and behold who hath created these things, that bringeth out
    their host by number: he calleth them all by names by the greatness
    of his might, for that he is strong in power; not one faileth (Isaiah
    40: 25-26). [10]The four and twenty elders fall down before him that
    sat on the throne, and worship him that liveth forever and ever, and
    cast their crown before the throne, saying [11]Thou art worthy, O
    Lord, to receive glory and honour and power: for thou hast created
    all things, and for thy pleasure they are and were created (Revelation
    4: 10-11). It is by faith that we believe that Jesus is the Son of God
    who died for the sins of the whole world because we were not there
    when he died, but our spirit bear witness within us that it is true.

    It is through faith that God created the world; the Bible tells us so.
    That we were made in his image and likeness, this makes it possible
    for us to operate in faith as he has given to every man the measure of
    faith. God is faith God and he expects every child of his to express
    their faith through his word. You must put your faith to work!

    But WITHOUT FAITH, IT IS IMPOSSIBLE TO PLEASE GOD:
    for him that cometh to God must believe that he is, and that he is a
    rewarder of them that diligently seek him.

    (Hebrews 11:6)

    And he that doubteth is damned if he eats, because he eateth not of
    faith: for WHATSOEVER IS NOT OF FAITH IS SIN.

    (Romans 14:23b)

CHUCKS UZONWANNE

Summary
of
'Why Do We Need Faith?'

Romans 5:1-2
Galatians 3:26
Ephesians 3:17
Galatians 2:20

Hebrews 10:38
Romans 1:17
1 John 5:4
Hebrews 11:6
Romans 14:23

How Does Faith Come?

SO THEN FAITH COMETH BY HEARING, AND HEARING
BY THE WORD OF GOD.

(Romans 10:17)

T HE ABOVE SCRIPTURE explains how faith comes to us—by hearing the word of God. Which means nothing outside of the word of God can give us faith. Obviously, in every human being is the measure of faith that is dormant until the word of God we hear is received into our spirit. This activates our faith when we do what it says because faith is encapsulated in the word. It is at the point of medicating on the word, that is, doing the word that we activate and exercise our faith, being obedient to what the word says to do.

This lets us know your faith is exercised when you do the word, and that increases your faith because what you hear always and think about, you will become, look, and talk alike. The Bible says as a man thinks in his heart so is he, and where your treasure is, there your heart will be also. Why is this so? Because the word you hear and meditate upon has been received into your spirit; it has gained ascendancy in your spirit; it is now resident in you, your spirit is its home, and with it, your perception of life has changed to become what and who the word says you are. You are transfigured by the word of God because of the power that is in the word when the Spirit of the word is unleashed.

And now, brethren, I COMMEND YOU TO GOD, and TO THE
WORD OF HIS GRACE, WHICH IS ABLE TO BUILD YOU
UP, AND GIVE YOU AN INHERITANCE among all them which
are sanctified.

(Acts 20:32)

God's word is Spirit and alive, and as we receive it into our own spirit, we are transfigured and metamorphosed into the image of him who created it. It has the divine capacity and ability to build and stir you up. It will energise and position you for greatness and success.

The Spirit of God's word will give you an understanding heart to comprehend, synthesise, and exercise your faith. It will grant you a vision of what your life ought to be and will help you live a glorious life. There is power in God's word if only you will believe it in faith and do what it says.

When you are in trouble, don't cry, and don't continue in confusion. Stop and apply the word of God to your troubles. Exercise your faith, because you're a child of faith; believe and see your troubles disappear, and they will disappear. That you believe does not mean the symptoms are not there. If you're sick in your body, but you are not giving consideration to how you feel now your resoluteness puts you at a vantage position where you can see and apply the knowledge of the spirit of God's word and receive your healing as you call it forth in the name of Jesus, glory to God! This tells us that symptoms are but a mirage that soon disappears as you approach them with your faith. They are false evidence appearing real; it's only a figment of imagination that is non-existent. This is what the enemy uses to put fear in people, especially those who are young in faith. He puts fear in them and makes them cast off restraint. I have often said that fear is a spirit that incapacitate the believer's faith, and that is the more reason, you must not in any ways submit to it.

If you are, for any reason, confused and don't know what to do with your life, that is, you don't know in what direction your life is heading—you have tried all else and nothing seems to be working—stop now and look up for a moment and hear what I have to say, 'it is a new day.' An inevitable day for a positive change, if only you would follow the leading of the Spirit of God's word. It is no time to cry and wallow in self-pity but time for a guaranteed positive change and all you need do is call on Jesus, the Living Word of God, and the Holy Spirit of God for direction. If you'd trust in him and patiently wait upon him to hear what he'd say to you and do what he says; he would put you over and make you walk in victory.

My mum used to say that fall down is not downfall; you might have falling down, but don't stay down. It is time for you to rise and shine by receiving the rock of your salvation, who will keep you focused on better promises to have all that pertain to life and godliness. I believe since you began reading this book, you can notice a change stirring faith on the inside of you, and you're feeling better about yourself. Your faith is being stirred in the right direction for your proclamation and possession.

Having inspired a change of paradigm in you for the journey of your upward life; your perspective of life now that you have put on a positive change must equally put on godly atmosphere by you studying and listening to the word of God on a regular basis until it gains ascendancy in your spirit.

Let it get into your spirit until it changes your thinking and perception of life completely, then you can bravely exercise your faith and bring a positive change into your life and be a winner! This is how important our faith is if we must overcome and take charge of the affairs of life. *This is how to exercise your faith for increase* by living and doing the word of God.

Summary
of
'How Does Faith Come?'

Romans 10:17
Acts 20:32

When you are in trouble, don't cry, and don't continue in confusion; stop and apply the word of God to your troubles; exercise your faith, believe, and see them disappear, and they will disappear, glory to God!

The word we hear is activated when we do what it says because faith is encapsulated in the word. It is at the point of medicating, that is, doing the word that we activate and exercise our faith.

God's word is Spirit, and as we receive it into our own spirit, we are transfigured and metamorphosed into the image of him who created it. It has the divine capacity and ability to build and stir you up. It will energise and position you for greatness and success.

Ah Lord God! There is nothing too
hard for thee.

(Jeremiah 32:17)

With God, all things are possible.

(Matthew 19:26)

All things are possible to him that believeth.

(Mark 9:23)

CHUCKS UZONWANNE

For verily I say unto you. That Whosoever shall SAY unto this mountain, be thou removed, and be thou cast into the sea; and shall not doubt in his heart, but shall BELIEVE that those things which he SAITH SHALL COME TO PASS; HE SHALL HAVE WHATSOEVER HE SAITH.

(Mark 11:23)

How Is Faith a Possessor?

FAITH IS A possessor because faith is a declaration of your meditation and the receipt of what belongs to you. Faith brings what you have called forth and makes you the possessor. The scripture says, 'Whosoever shall say . . . , but shall believe that those things which he saith shall come to pass; he shall have whatsoever he saith' (Mark 11:23).

This lets us know to exercise your faith; you need to speak forth those things you desire that you can see with the eyes of the spirit. You must understand they are yours in the realms of the spirit to possess them only when you can see them. And secondly, you must equally declare with your mouth to be able to possess them according to the word of God. This is the key to your receiving!

Remember, you must believe first for faith to take effect! Whether or not you receive is a different thing altogether, because when you believe, it strengthens your faith to see, to speak, and to possess, but to receive is the revelation and comprehension of the manifestation of your possession. This is putting your faith to work.

Summary
of
'How Is Faith a Possessor?'

Mark 11:23

Faith is a possessor because faith is a declaration and receipt of what belongs to you. Faith brings what you have called forth and makes you the possessor.

Receiving is the manifestation of your possession through faith. It is putting your faith to work.

For I say, through the grace given unto me, to every man that is among you, not to think of himself more highly than he ought to think; but to think soberly, according as GOD HATH DEALTH TO EVERY MAN THE MEASURE OF FAITH.

(Romans 12:3)

SO THEN FAITH COMETH BY HEARING,
AND HEARING BY THE WORD OF GOD.

(Romans 10:17)

NEITHER PRAY I FOR THESE ALONE,
BUT FOR THEM ALSO WHICH SHALL
BELIEVE ON ME THROUGH THEIR
WORD [MESSAGE].

(John 17:20)

How to Obtain Faith

1. Faith is a gift from God: This is the more reason why, above all else, we must be saved. It is at the point when we are regenerated (saved, born again) that we can understand the importance of faith:

   For I say, through the grace given unto me, to every man that is among you, not to think of himself more highly than he ought to think; but to think soberly, according as GOD HATH DEALTH TO EVERY MAN THE MEASURE OF FAITH.
   (Romans 12:3)

   For by grace are you saved through faith; and that not of yourselves: IT IS THE GIFT OF GOD?
   (Ephesians 2:8)

2. When our faith is weak and lacking, we need to pray to sustain and increase it. Our prayer and faith becomes effective when we maintain a constant relationship with the Lord:

   At once the father of the boy gave an eager, piercing, inarticulate cry with tears, and he said, Lord, I believe! Constantly HELP MY WEAKNESS OF FAITH!
   (Mark 9:24)

   The Apostles said to the Lord, INCREASE OUR FAITH [that trust and confidence that spring from our belief in God].
   (Luke 17:5)

3. Study, listen, and hear the word of God regularly:

   SO THEN FAITH COMETH BY HEARING, AND HEARING BY THE WORD OF GOD.
   (Romans 10:17)

And when there had been much disputing, Peter rose up, and said unto them, men and brethren, ye know how that a good while ago God made choice among us, that the Gentiles by my mouth should HEAR THE WORD OF THE GOSPEL, AND BELIEVE [HAVE FAITH].

(Acts 15:7)

And many other signs truly did Jesus in the presence of His disciples, which are not written in this book: But these are written, that YE MIGHT BELIEVE THAT JESUS IS THE CHRIST, THE SON OF GOD; AND THAT BELIEVING YE MIGHT HAVE LIFE THROUGH HIS NAME.

(John 20:30-31)

4. Listen to testimonies of faith: We understand that faith comes when we hear words that would inspire us and spore our faith into action to possess the object of our desire. We then must also know that nothing outside of the word of God can give such inspirations and move our mountain. So, whatever you hear if it is not of faith, I don't see how it can help you grow your faith. On the other hand, if what you're hearing is the word of God; I am confident it will inspire your faith for exploits.

Now Naaman, captain of the host of the king of Syria, was a great man with his master, and honourable, because by him the Lord had given deliverance unto Syria: he was also a mighty man in valour, but he was a leper.

²And the Syrians had gone out by companies; and had brought away captive out of the land of Israel a little maid; and she waited on Naaman's wife.

³AND SHE SAID UNTO HER MISTRESS, WOULD GOD MY LORD [Naaman] WERE WITH THE PROPHET THAT IS IN SAMARIA; FOR HE WOULD RECOVER HIM OF HIS LEPROSY.

(2 Kings 5:1-3)

The woman then left her water pot, and went her way into the city, AND SAITH TO THE MEN. ²⁹COME, SEE A MAN, WHICH TOLD ME ALL THINGS THAT EVER I DID: IS NOT THIS THE CHRIST? ³⁰ Then they went out of the city, and came unto Jesus . . .
³⁹AND MANY OF THE SAMARITANS OF THAT CITY BELIEVED ON HIM FOR THE SAYING OF THE WOMAN, WHICH TESTIFIED, HE TOLD ME ALL THAT EVER I DID.
(John 4:28-30, 39)

NEITHER PRAY I FOR THESE ALONE, BUT FOR THEM ALSO WHICH SHALL BELIEVE ON ME THROUGH THEIR WORD [MESSAGE].
(John 17:20)

5. We need faith to receive our healing and miracles and to exercise the authority we have in Christ. Healing was part of Jesus' ministry because God wants us healed. For you to receive your healing, you must first believe in the healing power of God; until you believe that God is able to heal you of whatever condition, you're not about to have it. You must see your healing with the eyes of the spirit and believe that Jesus desires for you to be healed. It is only on the premise of your believing and the exercise of your faith that you can receive your healing:

²³And Jesus went about all Galilee, teaching in their synagogues and preaching the gospel of the kingdom, and HEALING ALL MANNER OF SICKNESS AND ALL MANNER OF DISEASE AMONG THE PEOPLE.

²⁴And his fame went throughout all Syria: and THEY BROUGHT UNTO HIM ALL SICK PEOPLE THAT WERE TAKEN WITH DIVERS DISEASES AND TORMENTS, AND THOSE WHICH WERE POSSESSED WITH DEVILS; AND THOSE WHICH WERE LUNATIC, AND THOSE THAT HAD THE PALSY, AND HE HEALED THEM [Matthew 9:35].
(Matthew 4:23-24)

6. The Holy Spirit is the one that gives faith, healing, and miracles. The gifts of the Spirit are not for those who treat the things of God with levity, but for the mature who can comprehend the things of the Spirit, those with the understanding of discernment who have come of age and believe God to be the healer and the miracle worker:

TO ANOTHER FAITH BY THE SAME SPIRIT; TO ANOTHER THE GIFTS OF HEALING BY THE SAME SPIRIT: TO ANOTHER THE WORKING OF MIRACLES.
(1 Corinthians 12:9, 10)

I am the Lord that healeth thee.
(Exodus 15:26b)

The Lord will take away from thee all sickness.
(Deuteronomy 7:15)

HE SENT HIS WORD, AND HEALED THEM, AND DELIVERED THEM FROM THEIR DESTRUCTIONS.
(Psalm 107:20)

7. We need to understand that Jesus' physical suffering paid for our healing. There is, therefore, nothing, absolutely no condition that is too serious for God to heal when we believe and put our faith to work. Our faith only comes alive when we believe and stand resolutely on his word. Listen to what his word says concerning our healing:

He was wounded for our transgressions, he was bruised for our iniquities; the chastisement of our peace was upon him; and WITH HIS STRIPES WE ARE HEALED [1 Peter 2:24].
(Isaiah 53:5)

HIMSELF TOOK OUR INFIRMITIES AND BARE OUR SICKNESSES.
(Matthew 8:16, 17)

CHUCKS UZONWANNE

Many are the afflictions of the righteous: but the Lord delivers him out of them all.

(Psalm 34:19)

THE POWER OF THE LORD WAS PRESENT TO HEAL THEM.

(Luke 5:17b)

Ah Lord God! There is nothing too hard for thee.

(Jeremiah 32:17, 27)

With God, all things are possible [Luke 1:37].

(Matthew 19:26)

All things are possible to him that believeth.

(Mark 9:23)

Summary
of
'How to Obtain Faith'

---

1. Romans 12:3
   Ephesians 2:8

---

2. Mark 9:24
   Luke 17:5

---

3. Romans 10:17
   Acts 15:7
   John 20:30-31

---

4. 2 Kings 5:1-3
   John 4:28-30, 39
   John 17:20

---

5. Matthew 4:23-24
   Matthew 9:35

---

6. 1 Corinthians 12:9-10
   Exodus 15:26
   Deuteronomy 7:15
   Psalm 107:20

---

7. Isaiah 53:5
   Matthew 8:16-17
   Psalm 34:19
   Luke 5:17

CHUCKS UZONWANNE

¹In the beginning God created the heavens and the earth; ²And the earth was without form, and void; and darkness was upon the face of the deep. And the Spirit of God moved [hovered, brooded] upon the face of the waters. ³AND GOD SAID, LET THERE BE LIGHT; AND THERE WAS LIGHT.

(Genesis 1:1-3)

We having the same spirit of faith, according as it is written, I believed and therefore have I spoken; we also believe, and therefore speak.

(2 Corinthians 4:13)

How to Grow Your Faith and Keep It

DO YOU KNOW you can grow your faith and keep it on the increase every day? This is so because faith is spiritual; that is why faith is an unseen reality and the response of the human spirit to the word of God. With this in mind, we know and understand that the word of God is crucial to growing and keeping our faith.

We are also reminded that faith is spiritual and an unseen reality, which also means to operate our faith, we must override and completely come out of the shelf of human reasoning to embrace and operate in the realms of the spirit, thereby growing and keeping our faith.

Do you know why it is the response of the human spirit to the word of God? Do you know why it is an unseen reality? This is so because God has dealt to everyone the measure of faith; in every human being is God's measure of faith waiting to be activated and put to use.

Your faith will not grow until you use it! So use your faith if you desire your faith to grow by exercising your faith. For instance, if someone bought a car and does not know how to drive the car and no one else knows he has a car—evidently, he has a car because he has the key and it is parked in his garage and he can produce the receipt with which he bought the car—but it makes no difference until he is able to show everyone he has a car by driving it because not everyone will see the car parked in the garage. Some of those who see the car in his garage would say, 'But he doesn't know how to drive, so it can't be his.'

Even after he has learnt to drive a car, he still must drive the car in his garage as evidence to authenticate ownership. This way, he exercises his right over the car, and glaringly, everyone can see he has a car because he drives it.

The same inference applies to faith; your faith is there all right! But it will not be activated, grow, nor can you keep it strong until you exercise it. You must at all times exercise your faith; that way, your faith will grow and you will be able to keep your faith strong, because as you exercise your faith, it begins to grow on the increase unseen by your optical eyes, and evidently as you use your faith on a daily basis, it gets stronger and stronger, glory be to God.

Faith is not faith until you prove that your faith is working! How do you prove that your faith is working? You must believe and speak and be resolute in your believing once the active word is unleashed and released. The word you speak then becomes like the good marks man arrow that does not miss its target. The dynamism of the word becomes evident by its tremendous ability to recreate its kind. This is what faith is; the dynamic ability to recreate what you see in the realms of the spirit that the word of God affirms in the physical realm.

2 Corinthians 4:13 explain further. It is written: 'I believed; therefore I have spoken.' With that same spirit of faith, we also believe and therefore speak.

Being resolute is not getting unnecessarily anxious, worried or fidgety, but standing immoveable and uncompromisingly on the immutable word, and promises, and character of the One who created it. It is being persuaded beyond human reasoning that God is who he is; therefore, his word will not return unaccomplished or fall to the ground because it has the ability to reproduce its kind.

So faith is the creative ability that changes situations, in that, the principle of faith is God's principle of creation, which is the essence of life. In other words, faith is the inherent nature of the Spirit of life that gives birth to the spoken word of God.

> [1]In the beginning God created the heavens and the earth; [2]And the earth was without form, and void; and darkness was upon the face of the deep. And the Spirit of God moved [hovered, brooded] upon the face of the waters. [3]AND GOD SAID, LET THERE BE LIGHT; AND THERE WAS LIGHT.
>
> (Genesis 1:1-3)

> NOW FAITH is the substance of things hoped for; the evidence of things not seen.
>
> (Hebrews 11:1)

Faith responds to the spoken word and calls it into existence; this explains why it is the response of the human spirit to the word of God. One can conclude, therefore, that faith is inherent force that thrives in the face of opposition and encourages beyond what the optical eyes can grasp or comprehend. It transcends every sense of human reasoning.

CHUCKS UZONWANNE

Summary
of
'How to Grow Your Faith and Keep It'

---

2 Corinthians 4:13
Genesis 1:1-3
Hebrews 11:1

The word of God is crucial to growing and keeping our faith.
The principle of faith is God's principle of creation, which is the
essence of life.

Your faith will not grow until you use it! Faith is not faith until you
prove that your faith is working!

How do you prove that your faith is working? You must believe and
speak by being resolute in your believing once the active word is
activated and released.

Therefore having been justified by faith,
we have peace with God through our
Lord Jesus Christ.

(Romans 5:1)

And Jesus said to them, why are you fearful,
O you of LITTLE FAITH?

(Matthew 8:26)

Different Types of Faith

THE REALM OF faith is the realms of God's existence which is the realms of the Spirit. With faith, we are justified and can understand the operations of the Spirit of God. And it is with faith that we're truly in consonance and have peace with God. If we claim to have a relationship with God, then it must be on the pedestal of faith without which no man can believe, hear or see God.

The Bible says, therefore, having been justified by faith; we have peace with God through our Lord Jesus Christ (Romans 5:1).

This lets us know that we have been found not guilty and thereby acquitted and made free in Christ Jesus because of (the confidence, assurance, boldness) the faith we have placed in God through our Lord Jesus Christ, seeing that we have put off the unregenerate spirit (old man) with his deeds and have put on the regenerate spirit (new man, Christ), which is renewed in knowledge after the image of him that created him.

Our faith in God as believers is through Jesus Christ because he gave us access to stand before God justified, so by faith we believe that he (Jesus Christ) who knew no sin was made sin for us that we might become the righteousness of God in him (2 Corinthians 5:21).

The Bible makes us know there are different types of faith. The Lord Jesus talked about great faith and little faith, and Apostle Paul talked about weak faith and strong faith.

Little Faith

THIS IS INSUFFICIENT information from God's word in a person who tries to use his faith but cannot because it is not firmly founded on the word. It lacks knowledge and sustenance when put to work and wavers in unbelief, thereby not producing much result. 'My people are destroyed for lack of knowledge' (Hosea 4:6). What this kind of faith needs to be active is the knowledge and exercising of the word of God.

> Wherefore, if God so clothe the grass of the field, which today is, and tomorrow is cast into the oven, shall he not much more clothe you, O you of LITTLE FAITH?
>
> (Matthew 6:30)

> And Jesus said to them, why are you fearful, O you of LITTLE FAITH?
>
> (Matthew 8:26)

> Which when Jesus perceived, he said unto them, O ye of LITTLE FAITH, why reason ye among yourselves, because ye have brought no bread?
>
> (Matthew 16:8)

> ²²And straightway Jesus constrained his disciples to get into a ship, and to go before him unto the other side, while he sent the multitudes away. ²³And when he had sent the multitudes away, he went up into the mountain apart to pray; and when the evening was come, he was there alone.
> ²⁴But the ship was now in the midst of the sea, tossed with waves; for the wind was contrary. ²⁵And in fourth watch [between 3:00 and 6:00 a.m.]) of the night Jesus went unto them, walking on the sea. ²⁶And when the disciples saw him walking on the sea, they were troubled, saying, it is a spirit; and they cried out for fear.

²⁷But straightway Jesus spake unto them, saying, be of good cheer; it is I, be not afraid. ²⁸And Peter answered him and said, Lord, if it be thou, bid me come unto thee on the water.
²⁹And Jesus said, come. And when Peter was come down out of the ship, he walked on the water, to go to Jesus. ³⁰But when he saw the wind boisterous, he was afraid; and beginning to sink, he cried, saying, Lord, save me.
And immediately Jesus stretched forth his hand, and caught him, and said unto him, O thou of LITTLE FAITH, wherefore did thou doubt?

(Matthew 14:22-31)

Here was Peter trying to exercise his faith by walking on the water to meet Jesus, but something took his attention away from the source of his faith—fear and doubt. The Bible lets us know that he began to sink even in the presence of Jesus until he cried out to Jesus, and Jesus immediately stretched forth his hand and caught him. If Jesus hadn't reached out to Peter, he would have sunk into the water.

We must understand that doubt negates and nullifies faith and opens the door for fear to take over the human spirit. Doubt and fear are spirits that must not be allowed into your spirit because it will nullify the word of God in your heart. Jesus said to Peter, 'Come,' and he began walking on the water in faith made strong by the spoken word of Jesus as he received it into his spirit, but a distraction caught his attention away, he lost his focus, and in place of the word and his faith that was at work, fear and doubt took over and nullified the word of God sown in his heart and he began to sink.

Don't allow fear or doubt to grow in your spirit; always dispel fear and doubt with the word of God. Don't be a doubter, be a believer and allow the word of God gain mastery and rulership in your heart and in your spirit.

Summary
of
'Little Faith'

Hosea 4:6
Matthew 6:30
Matthew 8:26
Matthew 16:8
Matthew 14:22-31

Don't allow fear or doubt to grow in your spirit; dispel fear and doubt with the word of God. Don't be a doubter, be a believer and allow the word of God gain rulership in your heart and in your spirit.

When Jesus heard these things,
he marvelled at him, and turned him about,
and said unto the people that followed him,
I say unto you, I have not found so
GREAT FAITH, no, not in Israel.

(Matthew 7:9)

Great Faith

THIS IS THE type of faith that does not see opposition nor does it consider the outward conditions. This is faith in action. It doesn't have to see to believe and act upon. It is like the bulldozer that crushes everything in its path when put to motion and in forward gear. Great faith is a believer that thrives when all he sees is the end result of the active and spoken word. This is faith beyond reason!

> Then Jesus answered and said unto her, O woman, GREAT IS THY FAITH: be it unto thee even as thou will. And her daughter was made whole from that very hour.
> (Matthew 15:28)

> When Jesus heard these things, he marvelled at him, and turned him about, and said unto the people that followed him, I say unto you, I have not found so GREAT FAITH, no, not in Israel.
> (Matthew 7:9)

Great faith responds with an understanding of deep spiritual things; this is a revelation that responds with knowledge. Understand that when you act undoubtedly based on your knowledge of deep spiritual things, you are demonstrating and responding to a revelation of great faith. But in order to achieve this, you must be positioned at a vantage point where all you see is the reality of the promises of God. This means that there will be nothing of your natural senses that will negate or is standing in the way of your possession.

Summary
of
'Great Faith'

Matthew 15:28
Matthew 7:9

Great faith responds with an understanding of deep spiritual things, a revelation that responds with knowledge. It doesn't have to see to believe and act upon.

Understand that when you act undoubtedly based on your knowledge of deep spiritual things, you are demonstrating and responding to a revelation of great faith.

Weak Faith

APOSTLE PAUL TALKED about weak faith and strong faith:

> [19]And being NOT WEAK IN FAITH, he considered not his own
> body now dead . . .
> [20]He staggered not at the promise of God through unbelief,
> But was strong in faith, giving glory to God.
>
> (Romans 4:19-20)

Weak faith—this is when you don't act upon the word of God when necessary. You have faith all right, but it is incapacitated and inactive. This is the result of lack of exercising of your faith. It is not doing what the word says even though you have all the necessary information needed from God's word to move your mountain, yet remains inoperative!

If you have ever been to the wrestling match and beheld wrestlers; some of which are very big in size but inactive because they lack dexterity, energy and strength. They cannot stand the rigours of locking with an opponent because they're unfit, revealing their unpreparedness, and so they give in quickly in the middle of a bout. You can also liken it to someone who is very big in size without energy and stamina to run, when you ask him to run, will take two steps and start panting and gasping for air.

This lets us know, it is not how big your faith is but how active and how often you put it to use that will make it produce the expected results. If your faith is small as the mustard seed and active, surely, it will produce. Some people have big faith and at the point when they are needed, deflate so easily, and because they're weak faith, they produce nothing! Do not be like that; learn to exercise your faith and watch your faith grow to increase and become active!

Summary
of
'Weak Faith'

Romans 4:19

You have faith all right, but it is incapacitated and inactive. This is the result of lack of exercising of your faith.

CHUCKS UZONWANNE

WHAT THINGS SO EVER YE DESIRE,
WHEN YE PRAY, BELIEVE THAT YE
RECEIVE THEM, AND YE SHALL
HAVE THEM.

(Mark 11:24)

Strong Faith

¹⁹And being not weak in faith, he considered not his own body now
dead . . . ²⁰He staggered not at the promise of God through unbelief,
But was STRONG IN FAITH, giving glory to God.

(Romans 4:19-20)

S TRONG FAITH IS the faith that undermines circumstances but
fixes its gaze on accomplishing a giving task or purpose undeterred.
It is a go getter! This kind of faith trusts only in the promises of the Lord
regardless of what you hear, how you feel, and what your optical eyes see
and are dictating to your senses. Strong faith holds on tenaciously to God's
word, to his promises, and does only what his word says! And so I urge
you to strengthen your faith today and be a doer of the word if you must
have results. Practice and live the word and you will see your faith rise and
strengthened, active and operational.

Strong faith is the faith that speaks with the authority of knowledge and
it comes to fruition because it is graced with potency and has the ability to
recreate its kind! This is the God kind of faith with which he spoke creation
into existence and brought his meditation to fruition. God is faith God! Be like
him and be faithful. This is the kind of faith you need every day to move your
mountain and have victory and dominion in every area of your life! Whatever
your condition or circumstances, speak forth only the promises of God and
see an imminent change take place as you walk in the reality of his word.

This is how you exercise your faith if you must have faith for increase!

And on the morrow, when they were come from Bethany, Jesus was
hungry: ¹³And seeing a fig tree afar off having leaves, he came,
if harply he might find anything thereon: and when he came to it,
he found nothing but leaves; FOR THE TIME OF FIGS WAS
NOT YET.
¹⁴AND JESUS ANSWERED AND SAID UNTO IT, NO MAN
EAT FRUIT OF THEE HEREAFTER FOR EVER. And his
disciples heard it . . .

²⁰And IN THE MORNING, AS THEY PASSED BY, THEY SAW THE FIG TREE DRIED UP FROM THE ROOTS. ²¹And Peter calling to remembrance saith unto Jesus, Master, behold, the fig tree which thou cursed is withered away. ²²And Jesus answering saith unto them, HAVE FAITH IN GOD.

²³For verily I say unto you, that WHOSOEVER SHALL SAY UNTO THIS MOUNTAIN, BE THOU REMOVED, AND BE THOU CAST INTO THE SEA; AND SHALL NOT DOUBT IN HIS HEART, BUT SHALL BELIEVE THAT THOSE THINGS WHICH HE SAITH SHALL COME TO PASS: HE SHALL HAVE WHATSOEVER HE SAITH. ²⁴Therefore I say unto you, WHAT THINGS SO EVER YE DESIRE, WHEN YE PRAY, BELIEVE THAT YE RECEIVE THEM, AND YE SHALL HAVE THEM.

(Mark 11:12-14, 20-24)

Strong faith does not give consideration to the outward appearance of things; it is not deterred by any physical or natural evidences against the ability of God. Abraham is said to be the father of faith because he exercised strong faith and considered only the word of God by giving thought and attention and by keeping his gaze on the promise of God. He held on tenaciously to the word of God, which is why he staggered not at the promises of God but was strong in faith, giving glory to God even though there were physical evidences that negate his beliefs. He was not deterred. He only saw the word of God at work because he kept his gaze trustingly in God.

Abraham might have thought to himself that if God said it, he was well able to bring his word in his life to pass, and so he did not consider the deadness of his own body or the deadness of Sarah's womb, plus the fact that Sarah, his wife, was barren and past the age of child-bearing, yet he was strengthened and strong in faith trusting God and giving him glory.

I admonish you as God's righteous one? Live by faith! Go ahead and exercise your faith and put your trust in God. Be like Abraham and don't consider the conditions of your body. Let go of your past failures, and stop worrying about tomorrow! All you need for today and tomorrow is your faith. Be in control of your faith because it is within you; in your mouth and in your heart. You have the ability in you to make a positive change, it is all in your hand. Go ahead and exercise your faith for increase now and see all your troubles lose their grip on you. Then walk in dominion and in victory. But know assuredly, for all these to work in your life, the Lord Jesus Christ must first be the Author and the Finisher, the Perfecter of your faith. Give your heart to him, for it is the wisest first step to your victory, glory be to God!

This is how to exercise your faith for increase.
God bless you!

CHUCKS UZONWANNE

Summary
of
'Strong Faith'

Matthew 11:12-14, 20-24

Strong faith does not give consideration to the outward appearance of things. It is not deterred by any physical or natural evidence against the ability of God.

Strong faith holds on tenaciously to God's word and does what his word says!

God is faith God! Be like him and be faithful. This is the kind of faith you need every day to move your mountain and have victory and dominion in every area of your life!

Index

Nat Debt Line

0808 808 4000

b4 60days.

Ref: 3068753

0808 800 4444
Shelter